EXPLORING SPACE

Neptune

by Derek Zobel

Consultant:
Duane Quam, M.S. Physics
Chair, Minnesota State
Academic Science Standards
Writing Committee

BELLWETHER MEDIA • MINNEAPOLIS, MN

Note to Librarians, Teachers, and Parents:

Blastoff! Readers are carefully developed by literacy experts and combine standards-based content with developmentally appropriate text.

Level 1 provides the most support through repetition of high-frequency words, light text, predictable sentence patterns, and strong visual support.

Level 2 offers early readers a bit more challenge through varied simple sentences, increased text load, and less repetition of high-frequency words.

Level 3 advances early-fluent readers toward fluency through increased text and concept load, less reliance on visuals, longer sentences, and more literary language.

Level 4 builds reading stamina by providing more text per page, increased use of punctuation, greater variation in sentence patterns, and increasingly challenging vocabulary.

Level 5 encourages children to move from "learning to read" to "reading to learn" by providing even more text, varied writing styles, and less familiar topics.

Whichever book is right for your reader, Blastoff! Readers are the perfect books to build confidence and encourage a love of reading that will last a lifetime!

This edition first published in 2016 by Bellwether Media, Inc.

No part of this publication may be reproduced in whole or in part without written permission of the publisher. For information regarding permission, write to Bellwether Media, Inc., Attention: Permissions Department, 6012 Blue Circle Dr., Minnetonka, MN 55343.

Library of Congress Cataloging-in-Publication Data

Zobel, Derek, 1983-
 Neptune / by Derek Zobel.
   p. cm. – (Blastoff! Readers. Exploring space)
 Includes bibliographical references and index.
 Summary: "Introductory text and full-color images explore the physical characteristics and discovery of the planet Neptune. Intended for students in kindergarten through third grade"–Provided by publisher.
 ISBN: 978-1-60014-409-7 (hardcover : alk. paper)
 ISBN: 978-1-60014-681-7 (paperback : alk. paper)
 1. Neptune (Planet)–Juvenile literature. I. Title.
 QB691.Z63 2010
 523.48–dc22   2009038024

Contents

Neptune is a **planet**. It is a **gas giant**. It is made up of mostly gas instead of rock.

A **telescope** is needed to see Neptune from Earth. It was first seen in 1846.

Neptune is the eighth and last planet in the **solar system**.

Neptune

It is almost 2.8 billion miles (4.5 billion kilometers) from the sun.

All of the planets **orbit** the sun. A year is the time it takes a planet to orbit the sun. A year for Neptune is 165 Earth years!

A day is the amount of time it takes a planet to spin once on its **axis**. A day for Neptune is a little more than 16 Earth hours.

axis

Earth

Neptune is the fourth largest planet. It is 30,775 miles (49,528 kilometers) across. Earth could fit inside Neptune about 58 times.

Neptune

Neptune is very cold. It gets little heat from the sun. The average temperature is -370° Fahrenheit (-220° Celsius).

Neptune's **atmosphere** has many gases. Frozen **methane** gives Neptune its blue color.

The wind in the atmosphere is very strong. It moves at speeds up to 700 miles (1,100 kilometers) per hour.

A layer of liquid lies below the gases of Neptune's atmosphere.

gases

liquid

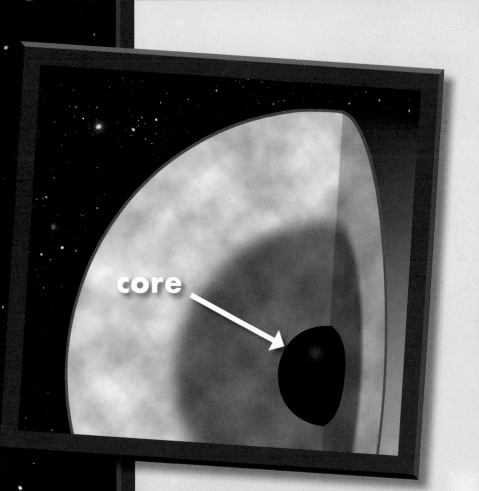

core

The **core** of
Neptune is made
up of rock and ice.

Triton

Neptune has 13 known **moons**. The largest is Triton. It is larger than all of the other moons combined.

Triton has active volcanoes. They shoot gas and dust up to 8 miles (13 kilometers) high.

Neptune has four **rings**. They are hard to see. They are mostly made of dust.

rings

Neptune has been
visited by only one
space probe.
Voyager 2 passed by
Neptune in 1989.

Voyager 2

Voyager 2 sent information back to Earth about Neptune's atmosphere, rings, and moons.

Future probes may orbit Neptune. They would send back more information about the farthest planet from the sun!

Glossary

atmosphere—the gases around an object in space

axis—an imaginary line that runs through the center of a planet; a planet spins on its axis.

core—the center of a planet or star

gas giant—a planet made up of mainly gas instead of rock

methane—a gas in Neptune's atmosphere; methane gives Neptune its blue color.

moons—space objects that orbit a planet or other space object

orbit—to travel around the sun or other object in space

planet—a large, round space object that orbits the sun and is alone in its orbit

rings—flat bands made of pieces of rock, dust, and ice that form around a planet; rings look solid from far away.

solar system—the sun and the objects that orbit it; the solar system has planets, moons, comets, and asteroids.

space probe—a spacecraft that explores planets and other space objects and sends information back to Earth; space probes do not carry people.

telescope—a tool that makes faraway objects look larger and nearer; large telescopes can see deep into space.

To Learn More

AT THE LIBRARY

Chrismer, Melanie. *Neptune*. New York, N.Y.: Children's Press, 2005.

Landau, Elaine. *Neptune*. New York, N.Y.: Children's Press, 2008.

Winrich, Ralph. *Neptune*. Minneapolis, Minn.: Capstone Press, 2005.

ON THE WEB

Learning more about Neptune is as easy as 1, 2, 3.

1. Go to www.factsurfer.com.

2. Enter "Neptune" into the search box.

3. Click the "Surf" button and you will see a list of related Web sites.

With factsurfer.com, finding more information is just a click away.

BLASTOFF! JIMMY CHALLENGE

Blastoff! Jimmy is hidden somewhere in this book. Can you find him? If you need help, you can find a hint at the bottom of page 24.

Index

The images in this book are reproduced through the courtesy of: Byron W. Moore, front cover, pp. 8, 9, 10, 11, 12-13; Detlev van Ravenswaay, pp. 4-5; Christophe Lehenaff, p. 5 (small); NASA, pp. 6-7, 14-15, 16-17; Richard Bizley / Photo Researchers, Inc., p. 17 (small); Science Photo Library, pp. 18-19; Mark Garlick / Photo Researchers, Inc., p. 19 (small); Seth Shostak / Photo Researchers, Inc., pp. 20-21.

Blastoff! Jimmy Challenge (from page 23).
Hint: Go to page 11 and shoot for the stars.